SONG of ESKASONI

donated to Norcroft by

gynergy books / Ragweed Press

1994

SONG of ESKASONI

More Poems of Rita Joe

RAGWEED
THE ISLAND PUBLISHER

Copyright © Rita Joe, 1988

Cover photo of author and granddaughter, Carla Jean: Caroline Julian
Editing: Lee Maracle
Book Design: Cape Bear Associates
Typesetting: Braemar Publishing Ltd.
Printed and Bound in Canada by: Imprimerie D'Éditions Marquis Ltée
Third Printing 1993

Some of the poems have appeared previously in *Micmac News, Tawow,* a Video Documentary produced by the Nova Scotia Department of Education and an Anthology published by the University College of Cape Breton.

Ragweed Press acknowledges the generous support of The Canada Council.

Published by:
Ragweed Press
P.O. Box 2023
Charlottetown, P.E.I.
Canada C1A 7N7

Distributed in Canada by:
General Publishing

Canadian Cataloguing in Publication Data
Joe, Rita, 1932 —
    Song of Eskasoni
    ISBN 0-920304-85-0
I. Title.
PS8569.03S66 1989   C811'.54   C88-098661-1
PR9199.3.J63S66 1989

To all native children
May the inspiration come to you
To tell your side, your story

Contents

Editor's Note

Poetry is both drama and song without the joy of music. It is life's unfolding in its essence. To discard a turn of phrase or re-write a verse of poetry not penned by the self can be hazardous. The inner spirit of the poet is violated somewhat by the carving of the editor's pen. Nonetheless, editing is often essential in much the same way that the body to be beautiful ought not be over-dressed; likewise the language of the poet ought to be as tight as possible.

In editing Rita Joe's poetry my own soul wandered across the hills, rivers and meadows of Eskasoni whilst my ear drummed out the rhythm of the songs of Rita. I heard at times the mesmerizing chants of the Catholic Mass and the sad drumsong of the Micmac. Both sounds achieve resonance when echoed by the voice of Rita Joe's soul.

Her Micmac spirit—her love of the land—peers through her strong sense of christendom and dominates her sense of spirituality. Rita Joe's poems pen for the reader that most important love of all—love of people in their quest for a just society.

Lee Maracle
August, 1988

1
To Be Poor This Was No Crime

Aunt Harriet's Waltes

1

On the floor of a house in Eskasoni
A blanket was spread for a game of cards.
The game they were playing, "What you got"
The last for a while, it was Shrove Tuesday.
A dime for the jackpot, only by chance
For them it meant much for winning.
Then no more the duration of lent
To the poor, this was no crime.

2

And in the same room
A folded blanket there lay
With two people on their knees playing waltes
While two more kept count.
The ancient game of the Micmac
Known throughout the pages of time.
It is just a game of bone dice and burl plate
To the poor, this is no crime.

3

Then through the door the mounties came
All authority, loud and power.
They gathered all the evidence
Sending fear to the unassuming.
The material for the reasoning was the dime
The dice and burl plate of waltes
The certification of a wrong to the public
To the poor, this was no crime.

4

Today, in the Regina archives of man
On show is Aunt Harriet's waltes
Created from bone and burl.
But I doubt they present the dime.
For unrecorded are the wrongs of man
To his fellowman who gave all
I record, so you may see
To the poor, this was never a crime.

The Children of Saskatchewan

In my native dress I stood before them
The children of Saskatchewan.
With trusting eyes and eager heart
Their search for hope
The fires of lore we rely upon.

I gave them my best
The heart pouring out the sea of love.
My views concerned the Indian-ness
Their search realized
That it was there, not told enough.

Forever Poor

He spoke of truth, and lied.
Every day, saving face,
He spoke of trust,
Do this,
Believing,
It was done.

Giving,
We drowned in treachery.
Great father government,
Treaties we hold, until we are no more.

Set us free
This vanishing race,
Forever poor.

The Micmac Family and Children's Services

There are roles of conduct that stir the mind
And people sleeping a long time.
Why do they awaken?
They see a way:
Their thoughts breathe
Their words dance on the page
Their power to ease the heart
In lifting the soul to help
Across this country, this age.

There are forces in action
Calming the land.
Restoring the pieces of mother's heart
Comforting the lonely child's want
Replacing the need of the caressing hand.
And worth to a father image
He is needed, he wept dry tears
Restoring the image, to the rising generation.

They sleep no more
The way became clear.
In agreements of wonder.
Resourcefulness an art
And sometimes with help from yonder.
Mi'kmaq Ankweywatiji Wnijanua aqq ikala'tiji
    wla Kmitkmitkinaq
(Micmac take care of their children and place them in their
    own native domain.)

My Song

This is my life
The soles of my feet touch
The fallen brown leaves.
My soul in expectation
Of the Great Brave.

I am his Indian
And my native song
Echoes through the hills.

Old Woman

Nikmaq woman
Face of old heartache,
Betraying hurt
Her thoughts of children far away.

Crying spirit tears.
Her fingers restless
Desiring to create
Pretty things for grandchildren
To share dreams, love, happiness.

Look into her heart,
Walk with her
Before life ceases.

The Art of Communication
(For the teachers in high schools)

Eskasoni is my home, a place of peace and harmony
Where bannock and tea are served
To anyone who is kind enough to visit.
I speak Indian to everyone on my reserve
And English to others
A gentle touch of communication to all.
This is my home, an Indian reservation to you
A welcome mat is spread containing our hearts
Come share with us
See the expression of kindness toward you.
I grew up here.
And every time you see me smile
With a quizzical look on my face
The cry for help is there.
Teach me the art of communication
Because, I want to tell you about me
The Indian of today
The lonely stranger to her own land.
But always willing to meet halfway.
Don't disregard my hand if it is offered in friendship.
I was only a child yesterday
But I am expected to be mature and brave
On the battlefield of assimilation.
Please help me.

Today's Learning Child

I see the bronze hue of skin
The dark eyes flashing.
The arrogant hold of that stare
Into the dream of that softness of life
Just out of reach.

The angry hold onto the reality
Into determination.
To see the life of improvement
Someday soon.

The head is bent, the shoulders round
That force upon learning, commanding,
Until dignity nods.

We are different to this age
We rely so much.

Please understand;
The chisel must continue to carve an image
Because all our life has already been labelled.

2
Talking

"Step"

She was born in Boston,
A bundle of tan-coloured noise
With dark brown eyes, a rosebud mouth.
And that stare of animation
All mothers see and take part.

She grew to a pensive beginner
All curious and love.
The life to the last
On the reservation we know
All our lives.

Then the learning part beamed on her day
In sunrise to the meridian high.
With the oral tradition we use
The major way we get by.

A melody of promise to her need
To teach the young the seed.
What remains in heart we pass
To others a song of new
We yearn to be where dreams are.

Our daughter:
She followed the golden rule
To guide the moccasin we follow.
Unguarded where we live, but true
The majority is the trail we trod.

Maine Indians

I know we are different
Though we try to be like you.
We live in the world of make-believe
In the field or forest, desk or loom.
We live in your world of speed and roar
Of mental energy, and tomorrow's door.
We live
Trying to catch that elusive dream.
We live ahead of time, on a silent scheme
To achieve greatness, beyond or over,
To smother shabbiness
The rooted word that yesterday took over.

We live, not on a reservation
Or amongst our people.
We survive, at the edge of overman
Trying to do what is right
In Maine U.S.A. na ni'n Ni'kmawa'j
I am a Micmac.

Andrew's Art

A peeled tree limb
Sturdy straight
Was whittled into swirls
To flowery symbol.
The fragile work of art
Of time immemorial
Rekindles the Indian's honour
Of expectation from the earth
That two become one
Today, he lies there.

Axe Handles for Sale

In Barney's River he knew they stood
The white ash for axe handles
He made splendid.

The load of logs he brought home
Soon to be quartered and hewed on workhorse-bench.
Then carving carefully with a crooked knife
The simulated handles appeared in magic
Solidly held in his hand with might.

A few hours sleep
Then fiery spirit of ambition
Sandpapering the handles to smooth finish.
In dozens and dozens ready to be sold
The morning sunshine reflected his joy
The Indian and his trade multiplied his satisfaction.

A Red-Skinned White Man

I hop on a train, a bike, a Cadillac
With a briefcase under my arm on a plane.
My business suit of finest tweed
With cufflinks of traditional azure
My back is straight as I walk with pride
To a convention, relying on my wits.

I talk with confidence reinforced by a degree
Waving my brown-skinned hands
To emphasize a point.
But I go back home to the reservation
Being myself.
And my work is done for the day
Being a red-skinned white man
Expressing my dissatisfaction
The way our country is run.

Bernadette's Dream

"I had a dream," my daughter said,
"Of a star falling into the water.
The shimmering sparkles spread over the water
And I told my friend, this should not be.

"Then I looked towards our house
There were three windows, in the centre one
I saw the St. Ann banner
The five of my sisters and I had made.
It shone in the brilliant light, so very bright
I thought it would explode.
Then I wanted to go there
To be near my family.

"When I ran into the house
I saw my family standing there.
The exploded distance of time had happened.
But they were standing there
With the pieces of leather and the roses on them
From the drawing,
My fears were softened, but now I worry."

"The St. Ann banner," I said.
"It brought a message,
The dictation we do not know,
But whatever it is, it belongs to Nisgam."
A week later we knew,
A dear friend from the Grand Council had gone
To the land all good nikmaq go.

Nisgam — God
nikmaq — Friends

Young Girls of Eskasoni

They have rock concerts in the community hall
Dancing but not touching.
Eyes focussed on nothing special
And a shy contact with the opposite sex.
A friendly teasing with others their age
These are the young girls of Eskasoni.

On Saturdays and Sundays
They appear at church
Along with the rest of their families
With younger brothers and sisters
Trailing admiration, conformity inspired.
These are the young girls of Eskasoni
Soon to be women.

Most go for higher learning
Not knowing what the future holds.
But some are angry for their tomorrows
In a mixed-up flow of ideas, not in bloom.
These are the young girls of Eskasoni
Soon to be women.

That Damn Damn Alcohol

I held her in my arms
Her flood of tears soaking my shoulder.
I listened to her lament of reasons
The continuous row of excuses for her drinking.

My heart ached for the love I felt for her
Trying to solve the problem I considered ours.
She was my sister, I loved her very much.
But I could not convince her
That the many illnesses troubling her
Were the result of alcohol.
"No," she would say
"I haven't had a drink in a month."
I held her close and let her cry
Accepting the fact of what will happen and why.

I went home to my family and promised myself
I would tell them I love them every day.
That they are beautiful, ambitious, intelligent
All the things to lighten the heart.
The words of trust, faith, I love you:
To her there were none, only the bottle
And finally the end.

Today, all I have is a memory
A sadness I recall.
Someone who was a part of my life is no more
Because of the cursed alcohol.

The Roddy Song

1

When he was just three, he was told to go away
When he was of age, to Shubie to stay.
Then came the day, he was a man
I'll serve my King and my Queen and fight for my land.

The life that he lived, was for no one but him
Existing on dreams, that someday will turn.
To the better of life for the natives and him
The brother I love, the nearest of kin.

Then came the day he was ill for so long
Couldn't remember the words he wanted to say.
The fighting was on to the land over there
I'll have to go back and help all I can.

Wherever he went nobody can say
Whatever he did there is no record.
But inside his heart was the one thought in mind
To fight for his land like it was at one time.

The loss of the man who was hurting inside
The love that he shared we know it won't die.
It will live on like the memories of him
The brother I knew and now he is free.

2

The loss of this man affected many people
He was an uncle, a brother, a friend
One day he was around—we never noticed
Other days he was around—he bothered us.
But the one thing that will hang in the air
As long as the memory of him lingers
There was no help when he called.

He did not scream
he did not swear.
He never pestered anybody.
Gentle was his quest for help
to heal the sickness that ailed him.
Now he is gone, nobody knows where
My brother
who took a part of me with him.

My Brother Roddy Disappeared, Then Found

On November 28, 1980 my brother Roddy disappeared.
No one knew where he went, what he thought
What pain he felt, or if he was scared.

All through the years we wondered
Through discussions among kin.
Was he alive?
Is he dead?
Or just a breath away.

On August 25, 1988, the realization became fact.
He was found, where he lay down so long ago.
Deaf to the past, no wish for the future
Or extremely sad.

No one knows.

But through visions in our dreams he communicated,
Apologetic for leaving, expressing love to all.
He lived, he died.
Whatever he couldn't say on earth
Now he sends pictures in our mind's eye.

P.S.—Rodrick P. Bernard missing November 28, 1980.
Found August 25, 1988 on Skye Mountain, Whycocomagh,
Cape Breton, N.S.   Christian burial, Sept. 1, 1988.

3
I Lost My Talk

I Lost My Talk

I lost my talk
The talk you took away.
When I was a little girl
At Shubenacadie school.

You snatched it away:
I speak like you
I think like you
I create like you
The scrambled ballad, about my word.

Two ways I talk
Both ways I say,
Your way is more powerful.

So gently I offer my hand and ask,
Let me find my talk
So I can teach you about me.

Graphics of Life
(when they emptied a dam and found ancient writings)

The graphics of life are firm
Identity comes of view
Brothers we are
The honoured Micmac of Nova Scotia.

The erased trail across the deep
dry sea where people once lived.
A rooted dream
Taken away and rewritten.

The sketches of life show
those who lived
arose by toil
their shade left behind in picture-writing.

Stone Writings

In caves of stone the figures lay
a symbolic gesture.
From eons of migrant sketchings
relating tales of journey and stay.
Proofreaders of yesterday's mirror

The characters are like trees
spirits that tell of life.
Eyewitnesses to bygone milestones
tomorrow's gift to children
an impressive understanding of ongoing relations

How true you ask the wind!
How true you shout to the world.
Bend your ear to aura
The mind will see the true mark
left forever by rooted cry.

He lives, the man in folded arms.
He lives in the sketches of wonder
In red ochre, the sacred colour
of the original faces of stone.

Micmac Hieroglyphics

"I noticed children
Making marks with charcoal on ground,"
Said LeClercq.
"This made me see
That in form would create a memory
Of learning more quickly
The prayers I teach.

"I was not mistaken,
The characters produced
The effect I needed.
For on birchbark they saw
These familiar figures
Signifying a word,
Sometimes two together.
The understanding came quickly
On leaflets
They called kekin a'matin kewe'l
Tools for learning.

"The preservation of written word
Was in so much care.
They kept them neatly in little cases
Of birchbark
Beautified with wampum
Of beadwork and quills.
These were the Micmac hieroglyphics
The written word of the Indian
That the world chooses to deny."

The Mistake of Columbus

Once too often
I have wondered
Had Columbus gone ashore in Turkey
Would we have been Turkian
Or maybe Miobia.
Would we then have been Miobian?
Or even Panape
Would we have been Panapian?

Deduction lingers
On Columbus' mistake
We, the world's greatest contradiction,
somebody's mistake.
Yet, happy I am
that none corrected it.

We Are Who We Are

The people speak legends
Brave deeds told to the children.

The habits of old
Identifies who we are
Relating what should be taught to others
In gentle trust,
So that we may bring to reason
We are who we are.
No amount of undervalue
Will ever bend that road to nowhere
That you have offered, ever since you found us,
The gentle savage, the fur trader,
The simple soul to apprehend
Enclosed by advantaged.

We are who we are,
The closed pattern remains
The search made it a masterpiece!

Soapstone Carvings

Graceful soapstone carvings
alive with expression,
Heavy grey on blue black stone,
each an original.

Indian and Inuit
carve and hone.
Attracting a ready mart
of many nations.

Carved from legends,
fantasies and dreams.
Each telling a story
passed through centuries.

Kulpu'ju' and the Seven Micmac

The thousand million people asked the Micmac
Where were they going?
"To see grandfather Kulpu'ju'
He is the same age as the world."

The seven men walked twenty days
Until they came to a large wigwam.
On his side lay Kulpu'ju'
An old man they thought
Approaching gentle and quiet.

"I'm glad you have come" he said.
"I haven't been turned for two hundred years.
"What do you want?" he asked.
"I want to live forever," one man said.

"You may have your wish
Stand among the trees.

"What do you want?" he asked another
"To be a good medicine man."
"Take roots, the side you turn me."
The man did, a gift of medicine was his.

"What do you want?" he asked another
"A gift of running, to hunt, to trap,
A good worker and many other gifts."
They left, but on their way
They saw a tree, the one who wanted forever.

To their people, they brought the story
And of the one who stood as tree.
To each in turn, a wish came true
They are the ones who make the living for us
The legend lives.

The Legend of Glooscap's Door

There is a doorway to Glooscap's domain
Where you throw dry punk and fish
For his fire and food.
But you must not enter
Though you may leave a gift on stone
Waiting to feel goodness.
This is the way the legend goes
So the Micmac elders say.

At Cape North on a mountain you whisper,
"My grandfather
I have just come to your door
I need your help."
Then you leave something you treasure
Taking three stones.
This is your luck.
This is the way the legend goes
So the Micmac elders say.

At Cape Dolphin near Big Bras d'Or
There is a hole through a cliff
It is Glooscap's door.
And on the outside a flat stone
It is his table.
The Indians on a hunt leave on table
Tobacco and eels.
This brings them luck, so the story goes
The legend lives on.

Indian Talk

Jiktek
All is still.
Silence reigns.
Tepknuset
the moon
A month.
Nemi'k
I see.

So long ago.

Nmis
my sister.
maja'sit
she go.
Nmis, my sister
Nutaq, I hear
Wena, who?
Nekm, her, him, them.

So long ago.

Api, a bow
Teken, which?
Ji'nm nemi'k
Man I see.
Kwitn, a canoe
App kinu'tmui, teach me again
Lnui'simk, Indian talk.

So long ago.

Mouipeltu' (Membertou)

Chief and Grand Chief, 1550–1611

On trails across the endless sky
I run with ease on moccasined feet
And the clouds part as I pass by
My name Mouipeltu'
I am a Chief.

I am a Ji'Saqmaw
A father, a warrior, a medicine man.
Still a leader of spirituality
My name Mouipeltu'
A Grand Chief.

And on the ways across the sky
I walk the ways my people meet
Leading the way again and again through Christianity
My name Mouipeltu'
A Grand Chief.

(Grand Chief Membertou was the first Micmac to be baptized to the Catholic faith, June 24, 1610—the first aboriginal people in Canada to be Christians.)

Shanawdithit

(Pronounced Shaw-now-dih-diht)

She was born in Ktaqamkuk
Shanawdithit her name
To a family life like yours or mine
Of caring people
The Beothuks of Newfoundland.
And then her people passed away one by one
Endurance no meaning anymore because of strife
By the newcomers who must own all land
No matter the price.
But survival became her way, even venturing close
To these strange people who can hurt so much
But there were women who cared enough to feed her
Allowing her stay to earn her keep as a servant.

And then six winters passed
A strange man with kindness in the eyes approached her.
The wounded heart replaced by warmth
Of a father image, a caring brother,
She tried to please him, learning the language
The strange ways these people questioned her.
She drew pictures
Trying to remember the implements of life.
Always working, repaying the life spared her.
Until she became easily tired
Needing the land of her people, to be close
To walk where they walked. Feeling their spirits
In dreamland, their nearness, so close but handshake away.
Finally she joined them, in the everland of red ochre
Shanawdithit, the flower of the Beothuks
The last martyr of Taqmkuk.

4
The Motherland

All Instincts As One

The cardinal sunset reflected on water
Ruby clouds melting away.
The seagulls flashing manes
Fish gather,
Dusk is settling at the end of day.

In obscure places
All animals asleep
Alert for danger.

The birds nest their young
In the quiet wood
Undisturbed.

The warmth lingering
The earth's soothing song
For resting.

Legacy

Abandon my country?
Forsake my heritage?
I do not see the need.
My birthright began
This country's history.

Our Habits

The inherited habits fade away
Like the mist in the morning
Of the summer u'n.

U'n — fog

James Bay

We are arms that are dust,
Lips that are dead,
Eyes that see not.
Minds dwelling in the mist,
Alive only in spirit.
My grave you dare disturb!
Because you think me less,
Desecration serves.
My land you possess.
Need you more?

The Balsam Tree

She stands tall, stately, elegant
With swaying arms.
Her emerald gown in rhythm
Of her beauty she offers.

She stands there for me
With invitations of scent
Her fragrance compelling me closer
For her wares to line my wigwam for comfort.

She stands there for me
With invitations of a cure
Her musky pine aroma overpowering me
To cure my ills with her skin.

She stands tall, stately, elegant
With swaying arms.
Assuring my confidence in sincerity.
Her emerald dress in rhythm
Her beauty she offers.

Basketmaker

The art forms in mind
The production originates.
Imagination plays the tune
Where creation settles.

If the bloom is to succeed
The flowery must be in wonder.
For the viewer eyes the end formation
Of the task in mind
The basketmaker promises.

Project Pisuaqn

The women there
Create on cloth
The design of the Micmac
Of long ago.

They sew with care
With gentle hands,
The geometrics of life
The aborigine saw around him.

These are the curtains of tomorrow
Documents of peace
Between you and I.

Let us admire them
They hang in the museum of man.
A part of life to bring forward
The record of the past.

The symbols tell of virility
On the pisuaqn
Tracing a status across the land.
Now it is there for you to see
That I was the master of my own dream.

Pisuaqn—Indian Dress

Taqmku'k (Newfoundland)

With snowcapped mountains
Black spruce bewitching pine
Of crystal clear waters
Rocky land outlines.

Tall church steeples
With tree-lined streets.
Free outspoken people
Good-humoured persons meet.

Skyward haze
Obscuring the hills.
Resources forever luring
Men with skills.

And the river's murmuring serenade
Tempting hunt.
With shadows of maple leaf
Sport of freedom.

River rock hewed
Embracing inlets.
Volumes of standing wood
Our Canada's monument.

Homes structured
Into the hills.
Sloping views forming elegance
Beauty beheld my eyes fill.

Passamaquoddy Song of the Stars

We are the stars that sing
We sing with our light.
We are the birds of fire,
We fly over the sky,
Our light is a voice
We make a road for spirits
For the sktekmush to pass over.

Among us are three hunters
Who chase a bear.
There never was a time
When they were not hunting.
We look down on the mountains.
This is the song of the stars.

sktekmush — spirits

Whycocomagh

There was warmth and love here
as memories passed.
There was security in the home I left.
The years have quietly passed
All old places and landmarks gone.

I looked on the ground
Only a hollow there
Where the old house stood,
Now bare.

The hill behind
Where we used to coast.
The muddy land,
Where we walked the most.

Modern homes and highway
A continuing action
To which the gentle people of Canada
must bow.

The winding old road is all that remains
The church and grounds
Where my forefathers lay
Whycocomagh, We'kopa'q
the end of water,
and I Rita Joe am one of children.

Eskasoni

A winding bay embraces the land
With spirited hills a protection.
The giving seas and the prize
My hunger ease, lifegiving.

My joy is here on the reservation
Where my part remains true.
And the mingling of hearts
To perception role, unafraid.

We must move like the rivers
Moving and protesting.
Then the undertaking of our heritage is
Our history we continue.

Near Mountains, Waters and Trees

There are record hops, beaches, community hall and gym
Folks want entertainment, to each their need.
Our church with a shrine, we revere.
The leaders of our people, we respect.
Our land is here, as far as one sees
In Eskasoni, near mountains, waters and trees.

For instance, there is Eskasoni Women's Auxiliary
Our greatest wish is that it succeed.
The trades we know are a way of release
To offer our country our achievements.
If you pass by on your way please
Come see Eskasoni, near mountains, waters and trees.

Throughout the year, the hills are a view
Especially in October, like painted pyramids.
Through the year we hunt and fish
Depending on resources, that spell Indian,
Our land always gave, we remember
In Eskasoni, near mountains, waters and trees.

In the morning we awaken to the sounds outside
Seeing the beauty of water and the rising tide.
Listening to old folks telling stories
Of long ago, when the earth was young.
Their deeds woven into history
In Eskasoni, near mountains, waters and trees.

Bras d'Or Lakes

In the valley amidst tree-covered hills
The rivers run on nature's course,
Bras d'Or she waits
Patient, expectant,
Ever the motherland's producing source.

And the wigwam of a morning fog
Releasing the mist upon the land.
Like the whip-poor-will's early song
Security is the touch on nature's open hand
Allowing plenty since time began.

Canada, the Motherland

Beauty rules the heart of nature
Like splashes of hue in autumn.
The small leaves of the poplar tree
Charming our attention.

We listen to the Quiet
The spirit veil.
Nudging the wisdom that is asleep
Where we may draw attention and focus
The attention of masses
To our land we love
Kanata to me, Canada to you.

We see the shining softness of snow
Pillowing our walk
To the everland of green
So dear to us
Since the dawn of time.

We hear
The sound of environment.
The reality of life
Which is true.

The answer to all of survival
To be free.

Just listen to the Motherland
Accept the flow of thought.
The beauty will be there with its privileges
In simplicity we teach.

Waters

They have been here since the morning of time
These waters which make three-quarters of earth.

Whitewashed stones of grime
The food no end
And admired across the realm.

But fear and suspicion when they toss
The serenity felt when calm
Awareness when cold, inspiring valour.

There is no other element as cruel
Nor kinder to survive man's abuse.

Comfort to body when bathers cool
Pay honour to these waters
Their supremacy rule.

5
The Empty Page

The Empty Page

Tears fall on the empty page
My thoughts wounding the heart
The bended wish unheard in the night
For soul-searching in the darkness black
What will I write?

I have nothing to fall back on
No wrongs I care to cleanse.
The engraved yesterdays not anymore
Or modernism I care to represent.
My revolt in dying embers
Peaceful my mission, I awaken.

I need your help, more than I ever did
And you care to open the heart
For my restraining wonder I held back.
We meet halfway, me doing my part
and you listen to my dream
I care very much we compromise.

My tears fall on the empty page
And only the breeze of kindness
Will replace the smoldering wonder of a nation
The majority familiarize and approve.
Giving my people something to cling to
Apathy remove.

Tears will always fall on an empty page.

Warriors

The days have disappeared
and will not return.
Your history tells our children
what you want them to learn.

That the Indian is the violent one
The wars the white man always won.

History records about the men.
Aye! What warriors they were
To deny this never.
For in the earth they lie.

The bravery, hardships, their deeds
are but a myth, my children read.

What price to pay
They fought for us.
But this:
You do not record.

The warriors are past care,
the lies, injustices their fare.

Now, tales are all that are told
Beyond the letters in gold
Our children learn today
our ancestors were there.

The Great One knows
what price we paid.

The Indian

Aye! the pleasant visions
We redeem from memory.
Kept inward, heavy in mind only.
Then the muted sense of honour rises,
To engrave upon the mind
The greatness that was always there
Only to be told.

The broken trail
Withstanding the ages
Serves as an emblem we see today.
The Indian!
The fabled individual
Of the dominant history.
One hopes to sway to mend the honour
That he so richly deserves
The Indian
The aboriginal.

A Fallen Nation

Tonight we sleep
On rushes cold
Our wigwams burned.
Broken in spirit
In hearts bold
Freedom fenced in the future.

T'will end, this hurt
Pray the end soon.
Dear brave
Feed not on resentment
Days to come
In many moons.

Our duty is to love
To give,
The newcomers our land
They need places to live.
A fallen nation
To be our brand.

And you my brave
No word of pain, or vain regret.
A fallen foe though we
In yesterday's flight.

Indian Song*

I'ko' i'kan e'
I' ko i'ko i'kan e'
I'ko' i'ko' i'kan e'
A' kan u' tai e'

I'ko' kan u' tai e'
E' i'ko i'kan e'
I'ko' I'ko' i'kan e'
A' kan u' tai e'

Come home, come home with me
See, see me at my home
We live, we live just like you in harmony
Hello, hello, hello
I am, I am just like you
We love, we eat, we sleep, we dance and sing like you.

My song I sing to you
I am, I am just like you
The song says it all and sing the words like you
Hello, hello, hello
I am, I am just like you
The song says it all and sing the words like you.

The vowel sounds—English A, e, i, o, u
Micmac Ah, eh, e, o, oo

*When I sing the Indian song to the drumbeat in schools, I usually sing in English for the children who do not understand. I made up the words in English—they are not the actual words to the song. I was told the song is in Mohawk, but when I sing it for them they do not understand the dialect. The song has been handed down so long the mispronunciation may have happened.

Our Present Destiny

The stars look down and see me here
Walking the earth
Like they did yesterday.
And the water's reward was
The giving
Likewise the land.
And mother earth and father sky
They saw and gave.
Until we reached the present destiny.

Our Indian Culture

Our Indian language tells the world
That we want to be just me.
Or dress in Indian-design clothes
That we want to be just me.
Or take Indian herbal medicine
That we want to be just me.
Even basket weaving or other craft
That we want to be just me.
Or Indian food cooked or baked
That we want to be just me.
Or religion prayers and song in Micmac
That we want to be just me.
And all the dances imitating kojua
That we want to be just me.
And our evening song, just like yours
That we want to be just me.

Memorial for an Indian Soldier

An Indian soldier, a warrior same
Protecting land like long past time.
And the symbolic name of a forgotten
tribe—Kanata, my home.
For them I die.

How true! We shared a loss
The memories die
The mayflower my monument
and the melody of wind across my grave
my lonely cry.

I served you my country
I wept for my dead.
Name your rivers and the mountains
Name your land, my warriors dead.

Then I can say, the freedom call we did
The heroes we shared.
Their spirit home the balsam
Lest we forget.

Answer my call from the lonely grave
The mayflower my poppy
The wind my rhapsody
The land my monument.

The Lament of Donald Marshall Jr.

*Everybody knows the story about Donald Marshall Jr. —
how he served eleven years in prison for a crime he did
not commit. The sad irony of the whole story is that they
were both minorities, the one gone and the one accused.
In 1971 these two young people got together that night as
easily as any young people would. It ended in tragedy.*

*The hurt of rejection is sometimes there in our society,
the failure of some people who take part in it are the ones
to be pitied. They are the ones who are blind to love, human-
ity, kindness and compassion. I speak for the Indian, or
any minority. The pain of rejection will always be there as
long as people fail to educate themselves that we are all
the same. We are all one.*

How do we remove injustice? Try moving hearts.

Song

I have served prison term, with locks on the door
My pain it is known, it is known the world over.
On my heart's aching core, I didn't do, I was told
He was my friend
We are the same, we are the same, we are the same.

My hurt is not gone, the key is beyond
The pain that is known, it is known the world over.
On my heart's aching core, I didn't do, I didn't do
He was my friend
We are the same, we are the same, we are the same.

The pain will be there, as long as men fail
My hurt it is known, it is known the world over.
On my heart's aching core, I didn't do I was told
He was my friend
We are the same, we are the same, we are the same.

Engraved Memories

A pleasant thought to memory
We redeem from rooted course.
In places of contentment
We are familiar,
The silent honour of the senses rise.

But if it was hurting and wrong
We tend to shut it out of mind,
The depth of misery smothers the bond
We care to leave, no man wants
Noted, it dies.

These are the memories we try to sweep
Sorting the ones to engrave.
Encouraging the salutation
To teach you about me.
Where you now stand, I gave.

How Soon Will I See Greatness?

My fears unveil my longing
to possess the very important view
In showing you my world.
No longer made important
       —this year of the jet.

How soon will I be allowed
to be as great as I was.
My back as broad and tall as trees
       —the speed, my run.

How soon will I see greatness?
Even my dead, you shun
I want as much or greater than you.
The need to share like I've always done.
       I want....

How soon will I see greatness?
The major point of my life
the weary uplift of my soul.
Let me have my say.
The perspective will be my own.

6
Inside My Soul

My Home on the Hill

My home on the hill
of peace and contentment
with understanding inside the walls
and shared love to all who dwell in it.

The dream dwells on the occasion
that part of life it brought
airy, like a lost apparition.
The fancy of a pleasant thought.

Poles and tar paper
pine branches for the floor.
A lodging of my motherland
Fading like smoke.

My home on the hill
of an Indian reservation.

Hated Structure: Indian Residential School, Shubenacadie, N.S.

If you are on Highway 104
In a Shubenacadie town
There is a hill
Where a structure stands
A reminder to many senses
To respond like demented ones.

I for one looked into the window
And there on the floor
Was a deluge of a misery
Of a building I held in awe
Since the day
I walked into the ornamented door.

There was grime everywhere
As in buildings left alone or unused.
Maybe to the related tales of long ago
Where the children lived in laughter, or abused.

I had no wish to enter
Nor to walk the halls.
I had no wish to feel the floors
Where I felt fear
A beating heart of episodes
I care not to recall.
The structure stands as if to say:
I was just a base for theory
To bend the will of children
I remind
Until I fall.

Mission Housekeeper—Mrs. Susan Stevens

Many year ago, she taught children
Their first christian word.
In Indian, her prayers were often heard.
Once she was stranded on Chapel Island
Yet never felt alone
Three days she stayed, never giving up hope.
She busied herself and tidied up the ancient chapel.
The Island was her home once, she knew it well
Being a housekeeper for fifty years.
The oldest Micmac tradition honouring St. Ann
The patroness of them, since christianity began.
Now she is gone
We will not see her at mission time.
To the world's most famous grandson
Her end was a musical chime.
Just to see St. Ann to make her smile
Her churchbell rings forever in heaven
And her famous Chapel Isle.

My Husband, My Man

I first met him, he came knocking on my door
Looking for his cousins in Boston in 1953.
In time we married, a family we had.
I remember he worked in construction
Surgery attendant in a Boston hospital
An orderly in Halifax
A nursing attendant to Sydney we came.
From there he became a labourer
To construction again.
A Field-worker for Drug and Alcohol
A Band Councillor, an Iron-Worker
Even auctioneering after funerals
Working for others to ease their pain.
Then one day declaring the return to school
To earn a degree, Bachelor of Education
To me admiration became my day.
Though there were ups and downs
Our boat sailed along
To each of us, our children and grandchildren
Hard work for canoe and paddle.
Then if we make uneven waters, the going ease,
It is because of the man who came, giving his name
That precious knock on the door.
What we are today we earned
To better our tomorrows
Using the gift of love and his fair name.

A Letter to the Holy Father

I wrote to a person I held in esteem
Using words of eminent regard.
I beheld his image in mind's eye
My spirit weeping, holding firm.

I re-read my words
Trusting the anchor we live by
And aspiration became a grain
Bordering the coast of a silent spell.

He wants to see me, I am the poor
I am an Indian, thinking to myself.
He is a lover of humility and low
And I am the first of the gathering cloud.

I choose the words of peace and understanding
A welcome of greeting to our land.
And if I may see the shadow of his passing
I would remain the same, aborigine I am.

The Speaking Engagement The Day After

I came home:
No answers came from my study
The inspiration unsatisfied.

The pain was everywhere
The ambition cold
Left on the shelf.

Then the valour glittered fiercely
Venturing hope.
The dawn brought the breathless award
My telling told.

Encouragement to Write

I stand before the native children
Baring my soul about our culture.
I stand before them offering my last,
For that golden dream, and the ladder
We try to climb.

The maiden speech,
The dawn of that titled page
To open doors.

I bare my abilities to them
Stating the limits,
The all-important meaning
To tell our side,
The aspirations.

They listen:
A generation of cultural mend is born
I see it in their eyes
The healing art of smouldering interest.

Premonition

While at work in the kitchen
I heard a sigh,
Like a depressed spirit
Struggling to free,
And a sudden chill
Held me firm.

I looked at the sky
Through the window
Wondering, why me?
My question left hanging
While I remain rooted.

Then it was gone;
I wait.
The channel takes a course
And I never cease to wonder,
Why me?
Only the loss, I expect....

Prophetic Dreams

Hello dream! I need your word-painting
The unique conveyor of matter
I want the meaning of.

Hello dream! I need the allusion
My people spoke of
I want the theory to contemplation.

Hello dream! I need your assurance
The need, my fancies come by
I want the expectation to dwell on.

Hello dream! The secrets we see
Are that trail into the green I follow
The interpretation, my echo.

T.V. Re-runs

The pain of mind
The parallel finds me.
The reels of the term undisputed.

Doesn't knowledge turn aside
The harm it causes?
Or is it deaf to our needs
And the stain it arouses.

There must have been honour
Somewhere there.
The role of the Indian
Whose soul they bare.

The aim may bow our motion
The rhythm of stress.
Re-opening wounds
And the ever-reduced status.

Sticks and Stones

If words touch me unkindly
The deeds I fling to the winds.
Though my heart lies uncaring briefly
The spirit rises in anger.

So I trim myself to the storm
Until it melts away.
Then I put my best foot forward
Breeding me the woman of stone.

And brush away the vacant trivia.
Firmly rooted,
The touching has not yet
Blemished my heart completely.

Yes, They Loved Me

To be content with what we have
Comes to the value with what we love.

To be the daughter of Josie Gould and Annie
Their winded path, I pass alone.
My brothers gone:
And love comes across the void
Seeing the gentle trail in dream
I try to follow by clue,
E'e, Kesalipni'k na—yes, they loved me.

Don't Turn Away

I wear a smile when I spend the time of drinking
I play the field for somewhere joy is reaching.
The time goes on and I'm afraid it's stopping
Come stay with me, don't turn away again.

Don't turn away, don't turn away, don't turn away
I'm losing you.
Don't turn away, don't turn away
Because this time my promises are true.

It bothers me, when drug and booze are killing me
It bothers me, when there's no one else around.
Why do they leave? They stayed when there was drinking
Why do they leave when all of my money is gone?

Come stay with me, I'll be your friend forever
Come play with me, don't turn away again.
I'm so alone, my heart is slowly breaking
I'll be your friend, if you help me once again.

So hold me now, the world is slowly fading
The lights are dim, the bells are all around.
Your reasons there, I'll listen if you tell them
I'll be your friend, if you help me once again.

Two Roads

Song (Sung to the Drumbeat)

Two roads we go, there's no one else around
Two roads we travel, til happiness we find.
And when we find it, we try with all our heart
To make the best of everything
Two roads we try to win the game.

Talking

Each one of us travel on two roads, sometimes they are
good sometimes they are bad. But whatever road we even-
tually take we are the ones who decide. Sometimes obsta-
cles fall along the way we try to avoid them, sometimes
weaknesses take a stranglehold, we work harder.

Song

Two roads we go, there's no one else around
Two roads we travel, the most we look to find.
And sometimes nowhere, the answer we don't find.
And it hurts to lose on everything
The road not always there to win.

Talking

So the road which determines our value is usually the one
with the briar patch, the hard road proving to ourselves we
have what it takes to be a success.

Song

Two roads we go, there's no one else around
Two roads we travel, sometimes good and sometimes
        wrong.
And if we find it, we try with all our heart
Giving happiness to others
Two roads we tried we won the game.

My Shadow Celebrates

Though it was natural for me to create my leather dress
The beads and quill my ornamentation
You call it art.
It makes me feel wise with a sense of identity.

Though it was necessity I used bone, stone, and wood to
    carve my images
You call it art.
It makes me feel wise and a seer of beauty.

Though I created the mask for mystical purposes
The amulets my ritual objects
You call it art.
It makes me feel wise as my spirit flows with love.

My sketches have revealed the loneliness of fading away
The message passing the wind into all eternity.
You call it art.
My spirit shadow celebrates, "You have found me!"